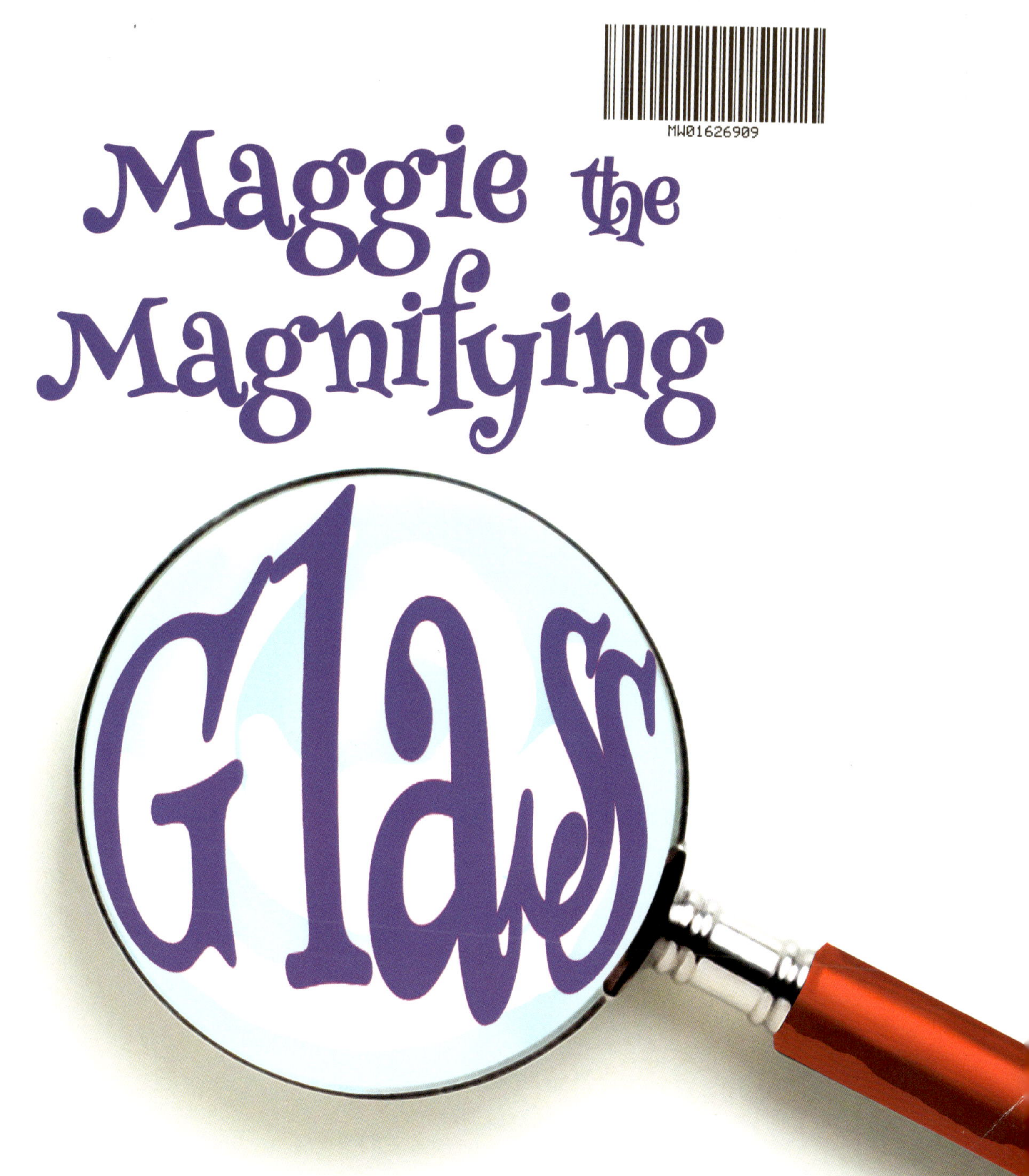

By Allison Bischoff & Jessica Yaira Gordon

Illustrated by Lauera Vanderheart

Hi! I am Maggie,
and I am a
magnifying glass!

A magnifying glass is
a tool that makes
small things look
bigger.

Being a magnifying glass is like having a special power. At school, I notice things that other kids can't see.

At snack,
the crumbs
under the table
look like
massive rocks.

During reading time,
the letters in my
favorite book
look huge.

I also use my super power when
Miss Rozzy gives us our class jobs.

Last week, I was line leader.
On the way to the playground,
I saw a cricket waving hello.

None of my friends noticed him, but to me he looked giant!

This week, I am taking care of our class pet, Lucy the Ladybug. It's my responsibility to feed her each morning.

During recess, I found the perfect leaf for Lucy to eat.

But when I opened the cage to feed her...
Lucy was missing!

My friends and I started looking everywhere to find her.

Priya searched through the backpacks, and Ben checked on the bookshelf.

We couldn't find Lucy anywhere!
Miss Rozzy told us that we need to think like scientists to find Lucy.

Scientists ask questions, like "Where is Lucy hiding?"

They also use tools, like magnifying glasses, to look at small things.

Are you ready
to be a scientist
with me?
Grab your
magnifying glass,
and let's look
for Lucy!

Let's check in the flower pot to see if Lucy is having a snack.

Is Lucy in the petals?

Now let's peek in the sink
to see if Lucy is taking a bath.

Is Lucy hiding in the bubbles?

Maybe Lucy is painting in the art center.

Is Lucy in the brushes?

Let's look on the carpet.
Maybe Lucy is napping.
Do you see Lucy?

See how fun it is to be a scientist?

After I found where Lucy was hiding, all of my friends asked how they could be scientists too.

I told them that anyone can be a scientist.

The best part is that there are so many different types!

Scientists can....

build bridges

or look at dinosaur bones.

They can travel into space

or develop new medicines that
help people feel better.

So the next time you want to be a scientist...

Get out your magnifying glass
and think of me, Maggie!